The Man From Snowy River

Poem by A. B. PATERSON

Illustrated by ANNETTE MACARTHUR-ONSLOW

COLLINS
PUBLISHERS

AUSTRALIA

There was movement at the station, for the word had
    passed around
That the colt from old Regret had got away,
And had joined the wild bush horses—he was worth a
    thousand pound,
So all the cracks had gathered to the fray.

All the tried and noted riders from the stations near
    and far
Had mustered at the homestead overnight,
For the bushmen love hard riding where the wild bush
    horses are,
And the stock-horse snuffs the battle with delight.

There was Harrison, who made his pile when Pardon
      won the cup,
The old man with his hair as white as snow;
But few could ride beside him when his blood was
      fairly up—
He would go wherever horse and man could go.
And Clancy of the Overflow came down to lend a hand,
No better horseman ever held the reins;
For never horse could throw him while the
      saddle-girths would stand—
He learnt to ride while droving on the plains.

And one was there, a stripling on a small and weedy
      beast;
He was something like a racehorse undersized,
With a touch of Timor pony—three parts
      thoroughbred at least—
And such as are by mountain horsemen prized.

He was hard and tough and wiry—just the sort that
     won't say die—
There was courage in his quick impatient tread;
And he bore the badge of gameness in his bright and
     fiery eye,
And the proud and lofty carriage of his head.

But still so slight and weedy, one would doubt his
     power to stay,
And the old man said, 'That horse will never do
For a long and tiring gallop—lad, you'd better stop
     away,
Those hills are far too rough for such as you.'
So he waited, sad and wistful—only Clancy stood his
     friend—
'I think we ought to let him come,' he said;
'I warrant he'll be with us when he's wanted at the
     end,
For both his horse and he are mountain bred.

'He hails from Snowy River, up by Kosciusko's side,
Where the hills are twice as steep and twice as rough;
Where a horse's hoofs strike firelight from the flint
    stones every stride,
The man that holds his own is good enough.
And the Snowy River riders on the mountains make
    their home,
Where the river runs those giant hills between;
I have seen full many horsemen since I first
    commenced to roam,
But nowhere yet such horsemen have I seen.'

So he went;

— they found the horses by the big mimosa clump,
They raced away towards the mountain's brow,
And the old man gave his orders, 'Boys, go at them
        from the jump,
No use to try for fancy riding now.
And, Clancy, you must wheel them, try and wheel
        them to the right.
Ride boldly, lad, and never fear the spills,
For never yet was rider that could keep the mob in
        sight,
If once they gain the shelter of those hills.'

So Clancy rode to wheel them—he was racing on the
        wing
Where the best and boldest riders take their place,
And he raced his stock-horse past them, and he made
        the ranges ring
With the stockwhip, as he met them face to face.

Then they halted for a moment, while he swung the
    dreaded lash,
But they saw their well-loved mountain full in view,
And they charged beneath the stockwhip with a sharp
    and sudden dash,

And off into the mountain scrub they flew.

Then fast the horsemen followed, where the gorges
    deep and black
Resounded to the thunder of their tread,
And the stockwhips woke the echoes, and they fiercely
    answered back
From cliffs and crags that beetled overhead.
And upward, ever upward, the wild horses held their way,
Where mountain ash and kurrajong grew wide;
And the old man muttered fiercely, 'We may bid the
    mob good day,
No man can hold them down the other side.'

When they reached the mountain's summit, even
    Clancy took a pull—
It well might make the boldest hold their breath;
The wild hop scrub grew thickly, and the hidden
    ground was full
Of wombat holes, and any slip was death.
But the man from Snowy River let the pony have
    his head,
And he swung his stockwhip round and gave a cheer,

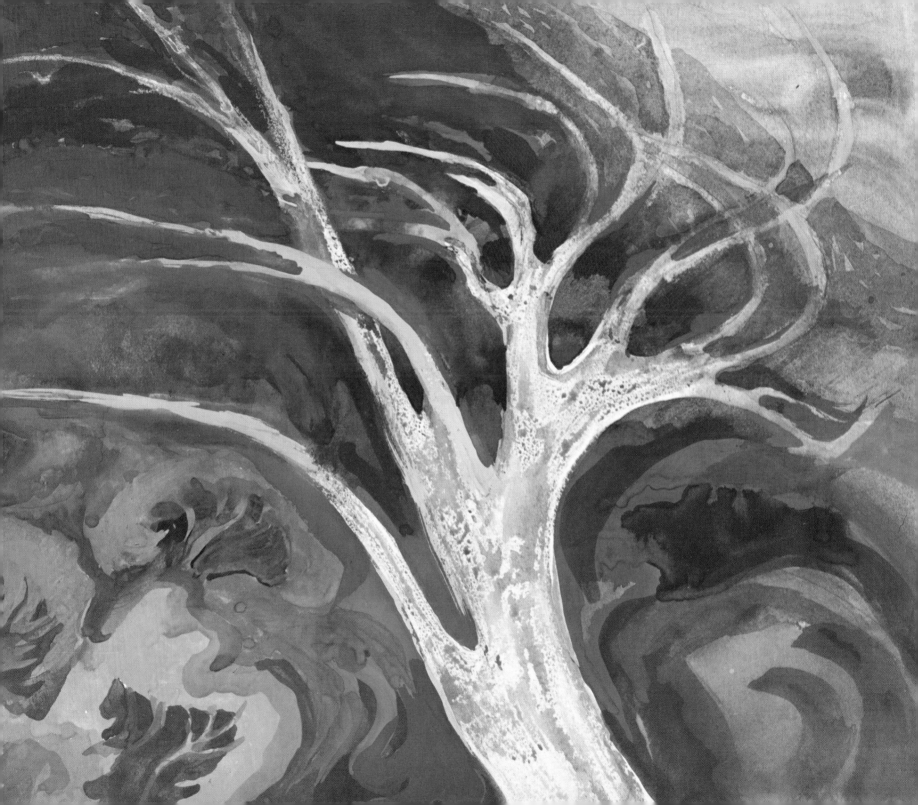

And he raced him down the mountain like a torrent
    down its bed,
While the others stood and watched in very fear.

He sent the flint-stones flying, but the pony kept his
     feet,
He cleared the fallen timber in his stride,
And the man from Snowy River never shifted in his
     seat—
It was grand to see that mountain horseman ride.
Through the stringy barks and saplings, on the rough
     and broken ground,
Down the hillside at a racing pace he went;
And he never drew the bridle till he landed safe and
     sound
At the bottom of that terrible descent.

He was right among the horses as they climbed the
    farther hill,
And the watchers on the mountain, standing mute,
Saw him ply the stockwhip fiercely; he was right
    among them still,
As he raced across the clearing in pursuit.
Then they lost him for a moment, where two mountain
    gullies met
In the ranges—but a final glimpse reveals
On a dim and distant hillside the wild horses racing
    yet,
With the man from Snowy River at their heels.

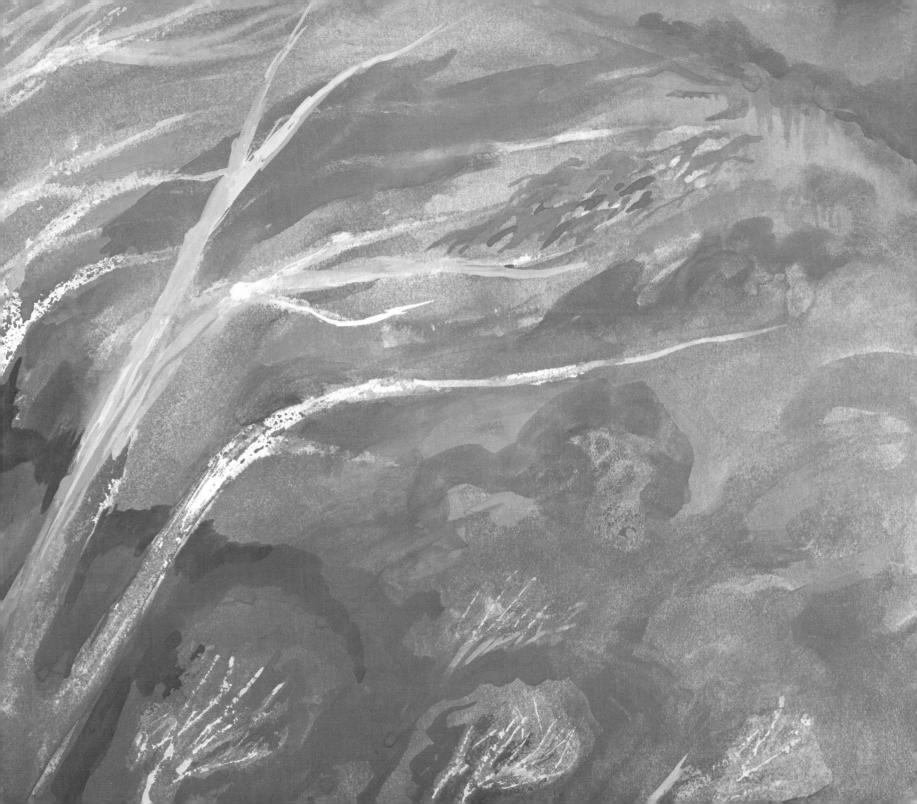

And he ran them single-handed till their sides were
    white with foam;
He followed like a bloodhound on their track,
Till they halted, cowed and beaten; then he turned
    their heads for home,
And alone and unassisted brought them back.
But his hardy mountain pony he could scarcely raise a
    trot,
He was blood from hip to shoulder from the spur;
But his pluck was still undaunted, and his courage
    fiery hot,
For never yet was mountain horse a cur.

And down by Kosciusko, where the pine-clad ridges
    raise
Their torn and rugged battlements on high,
Where the air is clear as crystal, and the white stars
    fairly blaze
At midnight in the cold and frosty sky,

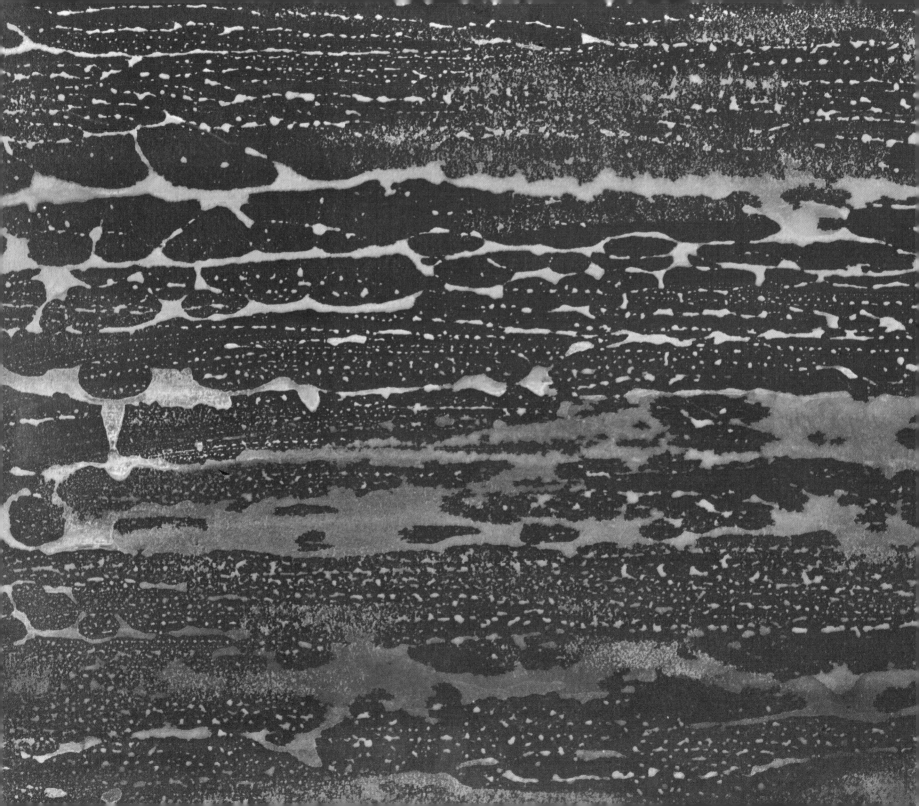